Flutter By

Flutter By

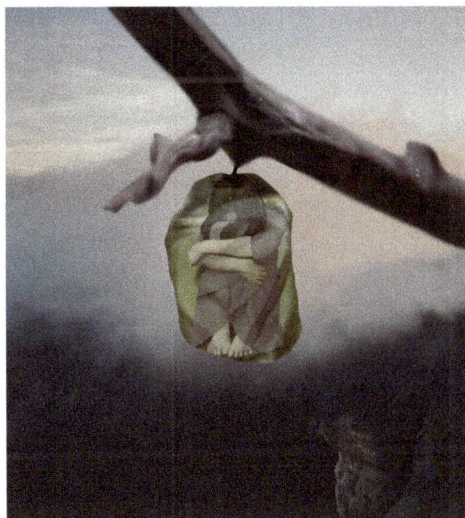

B. Miller

RESOURCE *Publications* · Eugene, Oregon

FLUTTER BY

Resource Publications
An Imprint of Wipf and Stock Publishers
199 W. 8th Ave., Suite 3
Eugene, OR 97401

www.wipfandstock.com

PAPERBACK ISBN: 978-1-6667-3132-3
HARDCOVER ISBN: 978-1-6667-2370-0
EBOOK ISBN: 978-1-6667-2371-7

APRIL 14, 2022 9:22 AM

Contents

II ~

III ;

IV ℰ

I.

The Director

Movies of the mind
produced by a man with shades
who sits on a folding chair and yells "cut"
more than he needs to.
Some are projected with a twisting reel
onto the wall of imagined thoughts
where a safe – maybe even happy – ending is discernable
through the binoculars of a stretched-out hope
appearing nearby, in reality far from it.
Departing the theatre, his feet land
on kernels of wisdom, dropped from popcorn bags
of the phantom audience who frequent his show
and now he's just a deer caught
in the headlights of one
horrible thought:
this film, it is false
a script of delusion
a trap of expectancy without any bait –
only his crazy, impossible dreams.

Jealousy

Just a brainchild, borne of self-denigration,
Emerging from a shell of pain and aggravation
And nurtured day by day in the crib of imagination,
Left to grow and fester with ferocious contemplation
Of the things it cannot have, will not acquire, life's limitation,
Using strands of self-doubt, it spins a horrible creation
Sucking up all joy, strangling all appreciation,
Your envy egg needn't have hatched but for its incubation.

A Name Humane

Hover over the globe, gaze down at our speck,
Understand for a moment what we forgot.
Mull over fresh blood, look aghast at the wreck,
All the throbbing horror that's been wrought.
Now answer this question we pose.
Is it not the mark of insanity?
That our species long known to be in its death throes,
You still call by the name 'Humanity.'

Button

Born with enough eyes to accept the threads of life,
Useful for binding halves,
Though tied down pettily straight in line.
Then to depart the fold, fall
Onto the floor, under the radiator
Never to be sewn again.

Worthwhile

They said the world was your oyster,
but you couldn't afford
the pearl, so instead the cloistered
oyster of your world clamped down
on your chest, which meant
the sand got in your eyes and stung,
flicked away your vision until
a single shoreline's grain seemed more
sturdily established than
you could ever be.

The March

When self-evident truths
Have evidentially expired
And the lines of science
Are blurred to misfire.
When the clumps of cells
Are too dead to voice
Their fear of termination
By the people of Choice.
For only the Chosen Ones
Are alive today
To walk the earth
And have their say
On whether you possess
God's breath within
And a one-of-a-kind pattern
Imprinted on skin
Or on when the divinity
Of a human's years
Will at least equal those of the polar bears.
When ears outside the inviolable sac
Have fallen deaf to a sudden gasp
As the prospect of feeling daylight
Slowly slips out of grasp.
When all of this happens
Out of blindness to the pain,
A word must be spoken
For those who cry out in vain,
With the hope that a single soul
Will be spared the knife
And so on that day,
They marched for Life.

Suggestion on the Sill

Are those eyes still enough alive to glance at the advice,
Retrieve an answer on the threshold of Inferno's door,
Beckoning its visitors – the sweat of your brow will suffice
Evanescent inconvenience, persistent toil is the cure
Impending Liberation waits for the quota to be filled,
There's certain life ahead when exertion's strongly willed.

May there be hope for their tomorrow,
And blessed return for this ragged mass
Could a solid promise ring hollow?
Have they not belief amidst the morass
To trust enough at the impasse?

Fortunate is he who knows the meaning of a phrase,
Reads between the lines and sees the smoke's billowing haze
Err not by the wrought ironic letters set in me,
I know and I remind you that only death will set you free.

Cents

Shuffles of shoes as heads
stare down at small screens
or shoelaces and up again at
the big screens, blank estimates of arrival
Dampness whistles by,
brings with it smells of regret –
should have gone elsewhere, missed it again
In a corner sits him, the giver of soothing sound
Delay is tolerable again
Joyful noise rebounds the walls, and
no heart is empty of the guitar's soulful strums,
which is not the case for its case
Some sense, begs the subway.

Saftie

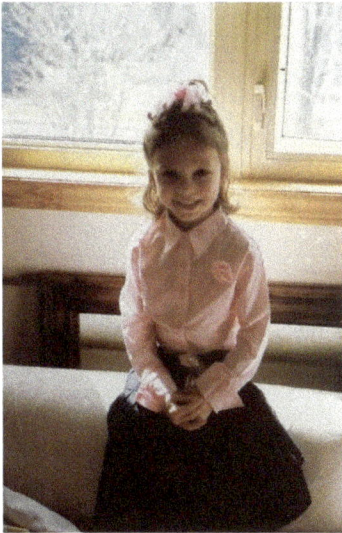
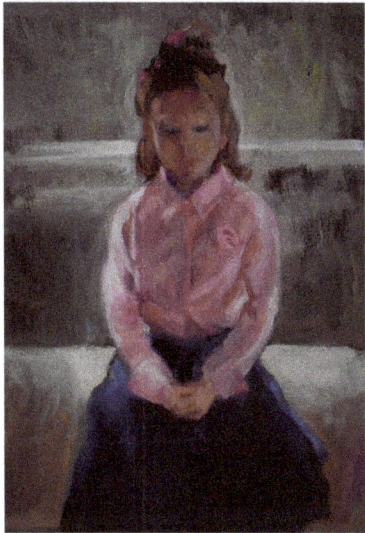

Small girl with a rash, standing against a door
the pain is soon painted within, inside skylighted studio space
on a canvas she now wears her angst, in that nightgown of blues
embedded in time

Flowers in a vase, there are plenty of those,
carefree father and son crashing through salmon waves,
and one woman on a zebra-striped chair, quite long is her hair
And there was me again, sitting on a bench,
reticent as ever

Three men interrupting, discussing
the shades of some shady argument
beneath the trees' shade in the brown heat of some day,
And there my Saftie sat bringing them all to life

So I tiptoed down the halls lined
with such varieties of moments,
of faces graced
with expressions
by pastels oily with solemnity

My slight fingers not wanting to ruin
those scenes,
I bounced on a chair and waited
for a chance to paint myself

"Here's a box for you," she finally said
and slid the pastels my way –
colourful lipsticks whispering the promise that
I could be an artist now too.

Sidewalk Sale

Mess to dispose of, objects to oust
from this address's attic,
from the members of this lonely house who plan
on moving out one day
A pair of strap-on butterfly wings for a kid who wants to fly
Radio Flyer wagon, A-Rod bobble heads, Ball mason jars, sunglasses –
four pairs
Pillows with elephant patterns, a Chinese room divider
Bowling shoes we never used, various nail polishes by Sally Hansen
Armchair: three generations old, ivory chess set minus its kings' crosses
Wind chimes bought at a Denver gift shop, they're a breeze
to assemble, as well as the IKEA table parts still in the box,
remind you of a puzzle, don't they?
Speaking of puzzles, there are fifteen over there,
No Missing Pieces guaranteed
The mobile that our child feared, a circle of lions,
empty calendars of past years
Red prices to mark the values
of useless paraphernalia, of cluttered unease
Please, someone stop at the curb
glance, jab, and
pine for the prize
you always thought necessary
to occupy your space,
just take it away and leave us at peace
And if we don't move away
and die here instead, you'll pick up our weighty remains
and bewail them – all expenses paid
Won't you?

Dragonfly

Magenta wings of a dragon
propelled by her dainty arms and
swept about the stage to the strains
of those violins.
At an agile slant is her neck posed
while her shawl falls and sways to lurching pace
as she glides, coasts,
weaves in and out of performers' swarm,
a molecule flung from center to curtain
and back again, when
the spectators glance, look askance
at the swiveling chair upon which she sits
to dance
with the two-legged dragons.

September's Sports

Those were her tennis shoes and
the racket she used
in her much-loved tournaments
before she left for her office.

That was his golf club, many a Sunday engaged
in the game he'd excel at, even more
than the financial wins
gained at the office.

Here are his baseballs, some signed
with beloved field heroes' ink,
the same ones that were tossed
by his capable arm towards his son's swinging bat,
to be hit higher than the stocks
sold in his office.

This is the latest display,
the glass-encased collection made
of the competitive ways that they played
outside of the office.

These were their favoured sports, their choicest pastimes
before time stopped for them,
before skydiving became
the new form of recreation –
from right out of
the office windows.

Inspired by the 9/11 Museum's exhibit
of victims' sports memorabilia

Bamboo Pantoum

Red highlights on stacks of notes:
They ordered us to uproot it all
Our shoots are sheets of steel
Devaluing their property

They ordered us to uproot it all
Illegalities of the clump species
Devaluing their property
Start three feet underground

Illegalities of the clump species
Insidious stalks are cancerous
Start three feet underground
But how? Can we afford this?

Insidious stalks are cancerous
Exploded pipes, ravaged foundation
But how can we afford this?!
Wall of nerves between neighbours

Exploded pipes, ravaged foundation
Our shoots are sheets of steel
Wall of nerves between neighbours
And red highlights on stacks of notes

Physics 101

When in time
they realized
the 4th Dimension,
that the Tower of Pisa
could fit on a pin,
for spinning atoms are all that
matter really is,
and what matters is
that they understood this.
As blurred blades of a fan
conceal multiplicity,
particles once thought intact
cooled down their egos,
betrayed them,
and that's Science.

Rummi Sub *(to be read both downwards and upwards)*

So, girl with a modest IQ, I need you to
lay out these colours just so,
honestly, you can get a Joker and
you know, maybe even win the game
Show me everything that
you have on your stand
the numbers
I'll make you understand
the rows,
and you'll go faster, contribute to
the tiles of impatient friends, notice them
here at our table
Frustration grows
What does she know?
as the pile shrinks, I think
I'll play for you now
Please just go

Photo Gallery

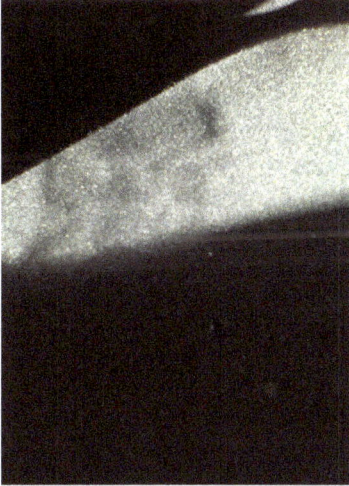

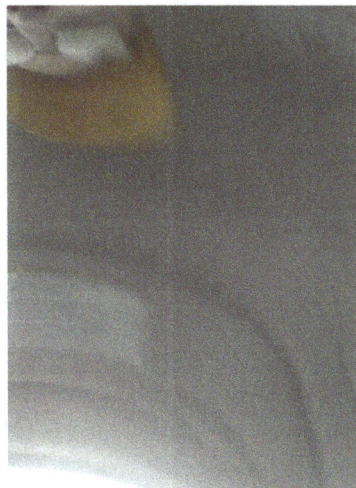

Pictures clicked
on a dead man's flip phone,
accidentally picked up
in the camera's zone
while shopping, he tried to dial,
but the price-match coupons were
captured in his grip
The basket was caught too, and croutons, he called her
to give him the rest of the list.

His eyes stare in an awkward sun glare
from glasses midair under his Wolverines hat,
Why *this* mistaken selfie is anyone's guess
Wheel of the car, his hand on a cloudy surface that
borders the glove compartment in the snap
He stares back at us now, his phone in our hands
Snippets from his wanderings, a cursory map.

He's asking, aren't you glad you found these photos unplanned
to remember me by in the errands I ran
The grey fabric on my front seat,
the drives to the store, and back again,
my belt buckle, red eye, black square from an unfocused lens
Good thing I clicked the cam button when I should have dialed instead
Now there's more to see of my life before
I spent the rest of it in bed.

Tenderfoot

A lady arrives to speak about her husband,
his death in a drunken crash
You'd think they'd care for a second,
they grimace instead
She cries for an hour and change,
then we leave the classroom to clash
our feet against the pedals, Juul smoke in my range
puffed towards my face, of all places, we're driving to Harlem
Swerve, nearly miss hitting my mom – heart attack
Who knew I'd be a matricidal one as I wildly come
around the corner – out of line, out of whack.

"I'm not taking my life for granted anymore!" says the freckled kid
Think he's referencing the documentary
on all those accidental deaths due to water, ice, skid
Parking lots and red lights are the only escapes
Honks eternal, my mind is off track
Jammed in a traffic pack, again my peers laugh
All I see are those who've perished in a road-slam smack
It's a Sunday afternoon,
and I'm out of my head
It's driver's ed
Enough said.

Record of Decay

They left me high and dry
They left me here to die
The children never come
They've got bigger fish to fry

When the world goes white
And recollections are hazy
I listen to *Everywhere at the End of Time*
To ascertain I'm not yet crazy

Some woman comes to play the piano now and then
The black hand on the white face reads gloom
I forget the tune
Reminds me of stale perfume

When once a sweet girl with braids came to visit
They told her, don't be afraid of this lady here
She's not all there
But she'll be your friend

She danced for me awhile and sang
I stared at the wall
Is that all?
In college I waltzed far better

My arms, they wave
The music fades
It seems the end is near
At least for my brain

Still I listen to those degrading loops
Of my life, the same old and new
The buzzing begins
Farewell, recollections
I'm off to heaven's queue

America the Dutiful

There will be friction if you say what you feel
Try to feel what we tell you to say
Or else we'll suspend you, blackmail you, or bribe you
For as long as we get our way.

There will be friction if you feel what you think
Try to think what we tell you to feel
Or else you'll regret that those feelings existed:
For too long you thought they were real.

Esoteric

Everyone thinks she is too esoteric,
Statements she's made make no sense
Ostensibly, clarity evades them,
They find her vagueness immense.
Everyone tells her, *be plainer,*
Repeat in a simpler way
If you imagine she listens, think again;
Comprehension is not her forte.

Squares

A side is completed, the colour is solid
No more Yellow to move to the top
He twists it again to begin the next side, but
The coloured jumble re-emerges with the swap.

Nothing is set as it was before,
Back to square one with this frustrating toy,
Front, right, up, right, up, front
Right up he *knew* this would be a killjoy.

After further rearranging, the Greens have been scattered,
But the Blues in his life are organized on the head
This cube of confusion only needed a compromise
To bring Green up before working on Red.

He now knows that when starting out on a section,
He has to scramble a path previously traversed
In order to reach the technicolour dreamscape,
Some perfect patterns, they must be reversed.

Life on a Cloud

Life on a cloud, so simple
Pure
Care Bears frolic here
The air is candy flavour

Life on a cloud, so peaceful
Secure
Nothing to fear
The sky's a violet glacier

Life on a cloud, so pitiful
Obscure
A restless sphere
The situation can't be graver

Note to The Franks

You should know you're being tracked, the annex is soon to be hijacked,
The writing on the wall, it reads so blatantly;
While you were sleeping, these eyes were poking, peeping
Your disregard for the Law is known – broken so flagrantly.
Time will tell when the informer shall spell
Doom for you and everything you stand for,
So here lies your final warning, they will be here in the morning
To cuff your sorry wrists and ship you offshore.
The slender staircase lends escape – forfeit now, and you'll be draped
In guilt and misery hitherto unknown to men;
Be intentionally ill-prepared for tomorrow's certain snare,
And your future will be robbed by Van Maaren.

P.S. Approximate arrest time: half past ten

Ilyich Kicks the Bucket

There once was a young man called Ivan,
Who assumed he would live for an eon;
He spurned love familial,
Was far too material,
And left the world with no shoulder to lean on.

II ~

Flutter By

The Creator completed the world.
He asked Creation's creatures
where best to place the source of
Love
and everything else good
in life.
The dust mite went first.
It figured it'd be a clever move
to position this gift somewhere under upholstery
where human skin cells could nourish
pursued legacies.
The lioness digressed and said
it should be the outcome of courageous endeavours.
The white-headed woodpecker ruffled its feathers:
"I disagree, it should be
put in the trunk of one's Family Tree,
a stem of hereditary qualities
in self-righteous succession."
The opossum opposed this:
"It makes most sense to leave it for
those who can build the most sheltered,
safe world
for themselves."
The sea pangolin
put forth its perspective:
"The fountainhead is perfect for those
who journey to the surface.
Where else would you
expect treasure?"
The bearded collie deemed
all the above folly,

since the good could only be
sequestered in passionate gestures
of camaraderie.
"These," said the Almighty, "are all fine ideas,
but they're all far too
Easy
to find, to vie for."
The Flutterby flittered near
and stood its spindly legs on the veins
of a lifeless leaf.
"I spend quite a bit of time
in stomachs that ache
from the mistaken search, in vain,
for the *It* that they necessitate
to bring them
Peace.
So here's a piece of advice
for all creatures who seek
to devise a way to hide
this source from
Humankind:
Why not conceal it
in the spot they'll never
think, suspect, imagine
falls within
their purview?"
And God agreed.
Which is why He hid it
inside you.

The Page She Missed

What he meant to her she doesn't know anymore,
any more than she knows why he went –
or where in the next dimension.
The grief was briefer than planned,
he's over, but what was it again? What were
those thoughts that stayed, cleaved
so strongly to form the idea of Him –
the loss he was supposed to leave.
What's left is stillness, nothing to ponder,
not much to sift through and use
to bring him back to life,
to form some need for his attention,
or to tighten the thread of their bond
that was thicker than a paper
withered and torn, yet
thinner than a silken bookmark
at the end of the story.

Spin Room

Again and again, it comes around
Then it moves away
Just like it used to do
And in the brutal slew
There's an answer for one or two
Of the Questions that were thrown askew
Spin, spinning, further confused
Avoid the crush
Pursue the news
The useless points
Of the Obtuse
It's warning you
It's warning you
Go get some tea in a back room
Decaffeinated, if that's the brew
That's right for you
That's left for you
That's middle of centre for you
(Unless it's true)
And when it's through
There will be no more place for you
To stand, to think, to hear
The View
The one you knew
Was best for . . .
. . . Who?

The Kahuna

Championship in Haleiwa,
And his dad grabbed the board, huge
And there was Isaiah,
Going through a sensory deluge
So beyond the routine shore
They roamed
First dip in The Insecure
The waves, they foamed,
But his mind went home, chose
The calm, whole, healing
Ebbs and flows, he held the nose,
The father, he was reeling;
One kid at a time, it will work
This water, the answer,
Stability can perk
From coast to coast, each camper
Will have a way out,
Out on the breakers.

Inspired by Izzy and Danielle Paskowitz,
founders of Surfers Healing

I Had a Hope

I had a hope, and the hope had me;
Then the earth opened up and swallowed it whole
Along with the pin that had held it steady,
Next the ship of alternatives was sunk by the shoal
With the wrapping paper and the guarantee,
And any last vestige of control.

Solitaire

Not ever quite enough,
Stuck in nature, uneven
Diamond in the rough.

A sort of developmental huff,
Late for every season
Not ever quite enough.

Somewhat crushed by the rebuff,
Just shy of an ice cut, beaten
Diamond in the rough,

Too transparent to bluff,
Few truths to weave in
Not ever quite enough.

Dark patterns don't show scuff,
The believer's yet a heathen
Diamond in the rough,

Not at all up to snuff,
Despair will deliriously deepen
Not ever quite enough,
Diamond in the rough.

The Russian Bus

The gown of the bride-to-be is stuffed
Under the seat
In case it gets noticed by
The Authorities
The boy who will be kept back
For lack of a student visa
Has no clue
The girl without any food says,
"I'll air sip your Gatorade,"
Sure, take it all
This guy falls asleep,
Lies across aisle,
Blocks path to bathroom
Crawl under, then
Vaping men
Gabbling girls
Weird sandwiches
Why couldn't we fly?
Breakdown in Monticello,
So off with all luggage
And onto the next (reliable?) one
Moonless forests on either side
Careen, 4:15
Finally, Duty Free
French forms to fill out in the dark,
Line up to answer
"To see grandparents for three days"
Glance at passports and travel letter
Next
Old man collapses
Seat maps of the vehicle passed around
For The Investigation

Mark down what was seen
It's 5:15
He's packed into an ambulance
Onward
No sleep, pillow is a burden
Pressed against the window by the
Head, arm, and leg of the large lady
Who smells and yells,
"How selfish of you!"
She's asleep
High-mast lighting poles, Tim Hortons, Mavis Tire
So tired
Mercedes-Benz showroom
Maple leaves, the never-ending, blurred, tan
Wall
And after all:
Cedarcroft lot
6:15
Zaidy's face's sheen
It's over

Waiting for Friday

On the waiting couch
For a while
For a while, juvenile
My unborn soul said so
What will be done there?
Here
Nothing to do
Definitely nothing
Except stay still
At the window sill, drops splash on the pavement
Circles in circles
Pools, orange fish dances and flaps his fins
Interruption One or Two, nothing better to do
Rewind the VCR
To the beginning
Black and white fuzz
Fuzzy blue hair
Wait, it's starting . . .
No.
Crackle off.
Black again.
Watch the wedding video instead
Watch four-year-old flower girl
Forget to stop
At the bottom of the steps
Wail as she's dragged away
Wait to be carried back there at the end
See the Torah scrolls
And then wait some more
My unborn soul said so.

Mist Understanding

Onions threaten my eye glands'
spill, it's a filmset trick

To cry on cue for the crew

See myself yet again, huge pupils
encircled by brown and boring rings
of relief: I shed tears too

What a day, what an evening
only to see it all close

Shut with the lids of hurried
yeses, nos, maybes even

Has me breathing, confused
as to why that mattered

Now I want to speak a syllable
to render it expressible, there should be

An explanation

The setting's natural:
just a space to watch the reasons
for seeing, thinking, being

Blinked away...

Into Oblivion

When the
A-bombs land, we won't know
what split us

We'll never
see the tip of the
iceberg, a Titanic

Carrying all
of Earth. Infants crying on
lifeboats that once

Kept friendships
buoyant between men. What will
down us in

The end? Heads
in sand as waves of
maydays hit

Quality Matches

They're extra long,
approx 45
not worn out

Ignite away,
keep distant from self
Stay Safe

This flame can kill
It will.
Abrasive surface

Content's
character is sticks,
they're quality enough

Do these strike you?

Suffolk Girl

Suffolk girl, Gabby Petito
Why is she gone,
and where did she go?

Florida fiancé, lost track of him
Living van life, not caring for his future
wife enough to say anything
But they knew it was something;
after all, she wore that ring
of his responsibility

Why on earth is this missing person
case going nowhere?
Justice is frustrated, the victim's a blonde,
bright woman

Now they found her remains,
it remains to be seen
what answers will be found,
what clues there are to glean

Suffolk girl, Gabby Petito
Why did she die,
and why's her boyfriend incognito?

Senescence

I wonder what it's like to age, with those veins,
Liver spots, etcetera, looking in the mirror
Going through the motions, feeling all the joint pains
Living with no regrets, fairness wasn't wasted,
Or actually, maybe it was; fake smile is pasted
On this old face staring back in the mirror.

"Is *this* what I look like?" peering from under the veil
Readying for the wedding in front of the mirror
How did this happen? the visage becomes pale
This rouge will not do, Maybelline will be superior
For a natural-looking flush and a subtle, golden exterior
I wonder what it's like to age by the mirror.

Fight or Flight

Such betrayal
Nothing left to do but pack up the
soapboxes and other stuff,
buy the ticket,
and be off
to another trippy city
Such betrayal
Much ado
about something
but nothing new
not a thing can surprise anymore,
be the Wizard when Toto pulled back the curtain
Such betrayal
Can there be a meaner
demeanour to bring it about,
a similar hypocrite who'd produce it too?
Probably not
" . . . please secure all baggage in the overhead compartments."

Poseur

Her eyes are windows to a worldly soul
Many suspend their afternoon strolls,
Pause to gaze at her glorious face
And her cosmopolitan clothes -
What a goddess of grace

A clerk appears, pulls her to pieces
She's reduced to parts in a box
Beneath the chiffons, tailored suits, and
Puffed fleeces
Her sophisticated stance fades

Seriously

The importance of being earnest,
it's worthwhile, I am told,
to always remain in passionate disdain
for any apathy towards life
and those notions
that one knows to be right.
To stay dedicated, fervid, and ardent
assiduous, committed, and staid,
it's really not rocket science;
seriously, why be so afraid?

Missing Heaven

His puppy whines
I miss you
Dry homesickness that comes from love
Deep, unexplainable
Even in a dog's age, he still has
Not found home.

Food Chain

The empty plate was laid before the customer,
his order was neglected, the establishment was understaffed
The others at the table received their meals and drank and laughed
A mozzarella basket, that's all that was asked for; the waitress,

                                                  he distrusted her

continuous claims it would be there any minute . . . of course,

                                                  the serving must occur

His glasses furious on his nose, it was obvious that trust in swift

                                                  service was as daft

as any fool who drooled thinking about undelivered food, and chaffed
those who thought they were better off with simpler dishes yet

                                                  quicker succour.

And spurned the need for *fast* assistance, since patience is a virtue;

                                                a piece of cake to wait,

to glimpse the relaxation of those gratified,
all the while with an empty heart, empty soul, and empty plate
to feel the pangs of hunger magnified,
and then to let the last of his nerves grate
over the lost hope of ever being satisfied

A Bachelor's Haiku

There is no harsh pain
like the pain of being so
lone for sixteen years

He said his soul was
so, so sad; a headache came
upon him back then

But if nothing else
he could have, he might as well
have God; he chose to

They were beautiful,
don't get me wrong, he remarked,
each in her own way

But the bombshell, she
left me with no feeling once,
there was nothing there

Most of his life has
been rides along the water
and then, not trusting

Until he drives off
into a ditch, God airlifts
him out, steers again

When he has to watch,
and play uncle, gets to both
hear and see their joy

While wanting those same
moments; *it's okay*, just stay
present for their gifts

Nothing beats little
kids coming down, leaping on
him when he awakes

So he lets it be,
like he is a kid again,
so playful, carefree

And eventually,
he knows the ride will open
to marriage's bliss.

God's Apocalypse

When the final pine cone drops to its doom,
And the barren wasteland sits cold
When the sun expands beyond its limit,
And when the young forget they're not old
When the fright collides with the unknown skies,
And the present basks in the rays of past shine
That's when the doubt will settle for good,
That's when I'll know that you're Mine.

Missed Milestone

The day that inches its way
invisibly along the strand
as a pulpous caterpillar
and emerges now and then
with enough wingspan
to carry it through
to the next year
Happy Birthday!
The smell of frosting
deposits a nostalgia
no one wants to taste
Happy Birthday!
It's the 29th of February
somebody bring out
the imaginary cake

Elevation Test

Sent a balloon heavenward,
perhaps a passerby who is considerate
will discover it and send it back,
or at least consider it.

Tied a friendly note at the bottom of the string
that said: write whereabouts you found this thing
when its rise had finally deflated,
do include all the details,
and be sure that it's dated.

Once that's all done,
remember to mail it,
and we'll both feel less lonely
Say, we'll both be *elated.*

Crowded

The conductor stood up straighter, stared
at the tired stream of people
for an endless ten
seconds
Shoved his numb
fists into his pockets,
gazed
mindlessly at advertisements
Braced himself
for the show of teeth
Punches of
holes in rows with no
gaps
Crooked ones. All the courtesies twisted, but perhaps for
an instant
they'd be straight
Sincere enough to appreciate
his existence

Elephants Can Remember

She held the recorder to their faces so they could say 'I love you'
They slipped it into the elephant, so carefully.
And she zipped it into her purse
To return to the hospital so their mother could snuggle it
And hear their last words
But hers, they'd never get to hear.

Mikvah Lady

Spiritual ritual bath at night,
The women come and go
The basement emits a tranquil flow
And is run by one whose careful sight
Ensures all aspects work alright;
Linoleum gleams, and cracks don't show
Walls covered with placid Van Gogh
She runs it all despite her plight,
And with no one to call her own
Still she lays out the soaps and flowers
In the hopeless heartache of her hours
Nightly the women file out, aided by her quiet role
And then upstairs she goes to sleep alone
She draws the drapes closed, she does not have a soul.

III ;

Archaeologist Bites the Dust

In a bed in Cape Town
the last picture in his mind
is not of the dirt –
mounds of dirt he's stared at, scanned
throughout his lifespan.
Not the dirt of excavations
to unearth a mysterious past.
To deal with faceless
History's past
was far easier than ever dealing
with his own.
Not the dirt of the grave
he's envisioned since the cancer
ravaged his pancreas. No, it's the portrait of the boy.
Would he come to bury his father?
He doesn't deserve that, he knows full well.
Perhaps on his final trip to the dust
he'll encounter the remains of his life.

Tribes

Tribe of kings,
what proud
masculinity
brings to the Round Table

Tribe of queens,
what grateful
maidens'
dreams are of a man

Toxic diatribes begone
'twixt all women and men,
rightful crowns don –
guide Eve to Adam again

Skeletons in The Closet

In the end,
they all were made
of high-grade
steel and plastic
frames,
plus unexpected silence.

Cavernous grins
with nothing behind them,
beatless hearts with
no remorse inside;
The bare bones were supposed
to remain undisclosed
until further notice,
or when questions were posed.

Docile Fossils

Hijacked minds crowded by cronies
Bereft of all reason, any semblance of common sense
A shackled planet saw at least ninety percent
Captured in a fog of phony perception
Condemned to a daze of lazy consent.

On The Fringes

Why do you wear those fringes on the corners of your clothes?
What meaning do they hold? What faith, what oaths?
To distinguish yourself as the People that everyone loathes?
Or to remember God's presence, and the verses He quoths?

Used To

This used to be a theatre
I saw *Cinderella* here the year that it came out.
That building there, it used to be my grade school
This strip of land used to be my daily route.
That apartment on top was where our tenants used to live.
Those synagogues were where we used to shout
While playing after services on Saturday
With the kids whose grandfolk used to hold a lot of clout.
This office complex used to be my workplace
Where I practised law and tried to quash reasonable doubt.
That house on Bison Drive, it used to be our dwelling
Before the one who used to be my wife
Decided to construct a sturdier, new one.
And that pretty much used to be my life.

Stranger Conversations

"Based in Kuwait. The hour is half past eight,
the oil's great." "Sounds nice."

On half the black boxes,
mics are closed; the other half are staring.

Does the Swedish one know the other Swede,
is this speechless conference some pressing need?

A quote to contribute, "close" impressions to spread,
though none are strangers to
the cues that go unsaid.

Forged

Held it up like a smouldered torch,
Gave it nothing but oxygen
Handed it off into the palms of
One God,
Gave Him nothing but company

And to witness the reckless undoing
of the cherry at the top of the please
wasn't too complicated – frantic passivity
Selected a nearby close second,
Rejected a far-flung seed, and
forsook the need to negotiate further: eventually a
burier can breathe

Held it up like a raging torch,
Gave it nothing but energy
Handed it off into the palms of
One God,
Gave Him nothing but companionship

The Grudge

Flagrantly waving the whitest of flags,
Gallantly having the gall
To show up in the middle of nowhere
With a four-years-too-late apology call.

Violently vying for a place in her heart,
Trying hard to ameliorate the shame
But no one said it would ever be easy
To appease the angst of a forsaken dame.

Final Reckoning

When the sizzle of the lamp casts its heat on the page,
The fragrance of intense study withers with the Sage
Heaven protests, the students face His rage
Stolen time will be accounted for.

When the hearts of the fathers return to their sons,
The narrow window to sight Divine subtly stuns.
The Omnipotent protests, they are the Chosen ones;
Stolen time will be accounted for.

When the might of the cavalry fades to anguished cries,
The donkey softly plods, calls to the universe: "Arise!"
No one protests, the nations see that Evil dies
Stolen time will be accounted for.

Possible to Plan It?

They say the moon landing was staged,
The rocks "brought back" were barely aged,
And the extent of this incredible hoax
Was much too wide to hide from folks,
Which is why they're here to inform us lunartics
Of the unlikelihoods of NASA's crude metrics
In other words, a thirty-billion-dollar swindle
Has for far too long allowed our hearts to kindle
With unjustified pride in that one small step:
Only a *giant* leap of faith would leave us trusting the States' rep,
And those 400,000 who worked on Apollo for close to a decade?
Yes, *all of them* were in on it when the "plans" were laid
So when you hear that God brought His Law to the mountain at Sinai –
Seen by some three million witnesses – that too was a conspiracy,
The perfect lie.

Lands' End

When Lands' End is reached,
Kindly send my regards
For now I'll be over here
Sweeping up the shards.

Where Waters' Start is situated,
Send me a sturdy boat
For once, I'll take up the oars
And set me afloat.

Or, whoever can find the Air
Of mid-level gloom,
Build a lighthouse right there
Reserve me a room.

Fishing

Merrily along, as if in a dream
To clench the stars' dust in a heap of perfection
Shallow waters don't bite, just deflect all reflection
Hard to swallow how to follow the stream.

Inkling of something deadly, thus far ... undefined
Cornered by a carrot – don't say I didn't tell you so
Stuck at gusty sea, and it's going down like Crusoe
Don't bother to dispatch saviours, ruin your daily grind.

Don't disturb coastal scoters by having them come
There's no reason to sink one's teeth in the hook
We're in agreement, so don't bother to look
For an answer to how you'll pay the ransom.

Eulogium

The whisper of a stutter,
A most hollow of affairs
The space between each pew
The space between each utterance.

Parted plumbly with unremembered energies,
Flourished in pruned, budded elegies;
Awash in melodious, affected sketches
Lines of tulips picked – pleasanter than memories
Seething with hyperbolic disease for deathless stretches.

Gushed forth with flushed exuberance,
Never did Respite deny fragments
Of pliant willow wonderings
Or sorrowful, empty laments
Kept dishonest by hushed coverings.

The hunger for more praise,
A most audacious wish
The lip service of glassy gibberish
The spurious verbiage given;
Bored all in attendance to death.

A Harvest Rushed Against a Setting Sun

Solidly morbid scarecrows stand still in the plane of quivering corn
Tightly survey the farmers' delight engendered by a pale, unripened crop
Slim pickings for a while, sights for soured eyes. *Patience,* throb vivacious
                            cobs – stagnation borne
of uneasiness; used to wheeze in an insect-strewn field left to the birds,
                            near hats of straw set atop
men's heads swarmed with despicable fears. *Where are the ears?* Still,
                    parchedly glisten at the roots' command: Grow!
But no Yellowed pulp, unlistening, squashed by its own masked glory under
                              heat reproachful
Shriveled, shriveled, dirt-caked; shadows of the garden rake hardened since
                            the morning's glow
Callow plants watched by the wastrels of all wasted pastures, enraptured.
                        Sown with vigour irrevocable.
Sweet air eddies, and the calla lilies expand faster, a burgeon punctual.
            Silhouettes set against a setting sun, stuck in freshly torn sod
hold paralyzed men in rows of confounded stares –
as the dare stiffly waits prepared for husks unsettled, forlorn, flawed.

Afterpiece

Gnarled strands
On the back,
Stubborn, slack.
Abhorrently arrayed,
Decoration did fade.
Showed a series of slip-ups and awful dye dips
Through all disastrous hardships.
For the Embroiderer has numbed all trust,
Stitching in the dark it seems,
In a design called misunderstanding –
Except the tapestry overturned shall prove outstanding.

La Dépossession

Poor fleur-de-lis,
I'll soon be history;
Charcoal bars surround to condemn
To the sabre, death by neckline hem.
There is no sense left.
That upturned look of my chin's cleft
Beguiles ingrates who wonder
How I'm still alive since the plunder
Of my château.
But they will never know
How the fractured statues of Judah's kings,
The jewels that lived in my signet rings,
The cartularies screaming in the library
As the flames ate them all, in their finery,
And the fresco of Jonah at the lips of the whale
Burnt to a crisp by the vicious canaille
Saw me off with a love that I'll never forget
When the whips cracked to beckon me to my debt;
So alas, let the carriage pass with the sentence,
The rich are left little in the way of repentance.

Bygone

Rushing towards an ice cream parlour
On the ledge there sits a man and his aide
"Where's the supermarket, woman?" There's not much time, she is afraid
But then he begins to talk with ardour
About the night of broken glass and the Third Reich's schemes
Delving into details that the devil left out
Of the Timeline – the man's a lost recounting spout,
The monologue won't ever stop, it seems;
The hour, it's running thin
Attempts to extricate from this
Sudden history lesson
Are continuously fruitless,
So to stay there and listen,
Be fixed to watch him reminisce,
Is the only cold option.

Heaven's Vanguard

Guiding Light in the afterlife,
Show them the dome of the highest dwelling
Speak about all that is seen beyond this,
And silence the angels with your retelling.

Don't darken the spirits or limit their view
Of the saddest story known to man –
Only remind those deadened to listen
For the deafening quiet that is God's plan.

Other Side

An eclectic collection of dust
Bunnies brushed under the door rug
Chain-link fence coated in rust
Strangers who walk by shrug
Guarded by a menacing pug
Crumbling to pieces of negative space
Curiosity politely tugs
Who owns this place?

Bicycles lean against the gleam
Of the garden gates
Rabbits under fountains' steam
Doormat freshly awaits
The homeowner's mates
Guest list is complete
And a fluorescent address locates
So they don't accidentally meet
Across the street.

And Now

It was only fair to be held by her mother
when she was born. Stiff arms were thinking, how
will this one have friends?
Something lethal ascends
the edges of her glowering brows.
And now antagonists are kin,
furtive quiver around each grin.
Everything went the way it was unexpected.
And now the professionals
believe in miracles because of this one
and say it's only fair that
the leftover idiocrasies be allowed.
And now three decades later
nobody hates her
or the way she did begin. More or less
blossomed to a nut, Meg, that
used to be her name before it was
Taken. And now, it's all
Goodbye to smileless "hi"s,
tree climbs,
and good lines:
she's driven off a road,
she's resigned.
Besides, she's fine
on her own.

Froideur

The heart
Came beating in
The wind
Kept banging
On the screen door
And all you were whimpering over
Was the lousy football score.
The frames
Were bending
Out of shape
Poltergeists gestured
Cornered your memory bank
And all you gave was
The faintest of stares – blank
Danker than the dampest day
This side of wintertide.

Inflated

Carrying a pot of boiling water
I saw a gold paper,
saw large dollar signs.
A bubble enlarged in the scalding water.
In my youth I counted every penny.
Now I see streams of figures.

Carrying a pot of frozen water
I saw a pink paper,
saw small digitized signs.
A bubble ruptured in the hardened water.
In my youth I swiped every card.
Now I see streams of breadlines.

IV ᘓ

Providence

As if there isn't enough
Room left, and it's strange
How fortune works
Its cookies. Never understood it.

Flakes collapse. They come
For me like glorious mares
As if there is no place for chance
Occurrences.

Awaken to snow in the room
Around the bed icicles curvet
My face glares from the crack in the
Wall
And all is well.

Grit

Grant patience, and grant it now
Fuller than this gravel will endow
And this sludge firmer than the hollow snails
Over which footprints have practised passing through hell
As a dashed lantern, as a desultory rhymer, as a tortoise shell
Hard, and yet slow. Yes, harder than nails.

Branded

Rang the sullen doorbell in vain
Stared at the obdurate panels, insane
Wooden barriers and railings made of pain
And a mailbox to carry an epitaph

An epitaph chosen by the one who was slain
A shepherd's last words are all that remain

Desperation runs through veins
Stillness scoffs behind window panes
In the place where all Abels met their Cains
And perished from a bloodstained amaranth

An amaranth plucked by the one who brought grains
A farmer in exile writhes in his chains

Dead Spinnerets

Weightless wisps of vagaries
You've stolen my gossamer.
Halcyon Araneae have all but vanished
As the future of a senile astronomer.
Left to a languor
Of psychic danger
Caught in labyrinthine labour.
Abdomen, glands swollen
My limber legs don't spin
The way they ought to.
Twist together every sin
You thought the wind blew.
Blew up the redolent flowers turned oranger
They eclipsed my handiwork
Further down I fell, and sensed the harbinger.

Espousal

She let her children play
with her wedding album.
Rip the pictures
out of the plastic,
sever them with peanut-buttered fingers,
cram them back in –
out of order, of course.
Her oldest asked, "Don't you care?"
She shrugged at the
streaks of white
from the rubbed-off ink.
One last photograph of them both
hung above the fire in safety.
One afternoon her youngest threw
a ball that knocked the
barefaced fireplace
picture off its hook.
It came crashing down,
a cascade of crystals.
She swept it up.
She threw out the picture,
didn't want to cut her fingers
extracting it from the frame.
When her husband came home,
he chuckled and hung
his workplace ID on the hook
instead.

The Move Down

A visit to somewhere I can't remember
Now, but it must have been fleeting as
I followed my father into the Room Changer
The sides slid shut. Triangles

Floated on the walls. My innards fell
Inwards. I didn't panic though. Why,
I don't know. Disorientation kicked in
Right away, I missed the feel of the other

Place. It was a foyer to a dollhouse
Or a pebbly playground, or so it looked from
Three-feet-high eyes. Trapped in that
Contraption again, but not taken by surprise because

That wasn't the first time everything changed
Hurled into a room with purple carpeting and wooden walls
Not realizing the switch would confront me
As the first room with the couch in the corner
Vanished as the cat by the window did in my
First nightmare.

Tinted

And there lay the daydreamer, wizened and cold,
Painting Pollyanna in colours bright, bold
With the sweat on his brow and ambrosian airs,
He sat there for days. Oh, he stayed there for years.

Until one balmily evening when the sun had just West fallen,
The nerves in his chest began to press, crestfallen
He'd lingered forever, an idealist so consummate,
And there lay derisory existence, disconsolate.

Deciduous Drowsiness

Seldom did it ever rain,
Yet when it did, a sleepwalker stirred.
With not much left to keep life sane,
The lawn sprinklers jolted awake,
The hydrangeas languished with ache.

Such a frivolous space, too arboreal;
Boredom trickled in roots
A ripple of interest
Until thirsty pulses ethereal
Clambered out of branches
And lurched over rumples of slumber in the seedbed
And beheld with reticence where a neglected deed led.
And after all this,
No somnolence, fortuitously, further pollutes
The most faultless of foliage.

Rest Your Want

Good thing you came late.
They had more time
To lay down the entrée you wanted,
Smells like this rendezvous haunted.
Crackers and water, milkshakes for dessert
Main course is anguish, appetizer was hurt.
And as
You watch him joke around,
Undecided, all the time in the world
To order,
The night breathes a sigh of
Good grief.
In brief, this life never became
Your maître d'.
Not the slightest bite was ever meant to be.

Used

"Come thrifting," she said with a lilt in her voice
Dragged our mitts through the racks,
None of it was a choice
Fine china stashed into burgundy sacks
Mustiness dried out
Rows and rows of raw honey
Mustiness dried out
The uselessness of money
Spent in that corner
Exploited to adorn her
No way to leave
Tunnels of waste
Dried-out mustiness
Tunnels of waste
Starved glutton
Coughed, a sudden chest
Heave
Heaved it all out
Quenched drought
If not in a week,
At least for now

Altar Waiting

Werewolf, why have you gone away?
Wild sheep wait underneath oaks
and falter to detect your bray.

Terror below violence chokes –
the splinter of a Leonid shower
that galactic habitat's tide provokes.

Frightened by asylum at a plateau
No antidote in the quagmire
quells the madness of the status quo.

Prey, predator on the spyre
both nibble on bedraggled dread,
for Transformations have all turned dire.

Faster than an affliction can spread,
both turn more rabid than disaster,
more static than the scare their howls bred.

Ocean Spray

Toy boat below the vent
Never will it journey
Never will it disturb me
With explorer's malcontent.
Borrowed most of what was spent,
Forayed into a wilderness as free
As a dove before it bled out at sea:
Ocean spray, it knew not where it went.
So all of us are wandering, not worth finding
Any more than a plaything or a bird
Stuck within the basement grate.
Ocean spray, it doesn't get more blinding;
No course to set or loins to gird
Or voice to reassure, *it's not too late.*

A Void Dance

Spontaneous equivocations
[Psychoanalysis has through desolate designations
Marked the lips
With practised disagreements
& Problems pronounced with slips
Of the tongue after a dream hints
To some perilous revelations]
Spontaneous equivocations

You Had to Be There

You had to be
there when the snow globe
overturned, and the miniatures screamed.
My dear, what a scare.
Shrieks flickered round each earlobe.
A tragedy
that you had to be there
to see
because believe me:
you have to beware.
Our stability's gravely
endangered
by The Shakers
lurking near.
Really.
They have got to
be here
somewhere.

Composed

draft without adjectives
resigned to the fate
of a blank slate
with nothing to say
what else is new
what else was there
to mention here and
chase suspicion away
no need to delay
the punch of keys
that crunch of ease
as if the screen
didn't freeze
deception is already
well underway

Reasonably Healthy

Reasonably healthy,
Reasonably so
Meaning, everything that went wrong
Found another place to go.
Truly, all that weeping was
Only the bleeding of
The soul
Congealing to heal, flowing to condole.
And really, resilience is all there is,
So not to worry to and fro.
Reasonably healthy indeed
That's what they said,
How did they know?

Rehashed

Before the silver linings
Thought to creep around
An early bird arose to
Chirp with meager sound
Muted kitchen
Frigid floor
Tiptoed to read the funnies
That were not funny anymore
Mashed the yolkless form
Poured a thermos full with scorn
Searing reminder, a morning
Unadorned
Walked out the door
Fumbled for some humour
Came up
Short
So in lieu of that
Sorted out all things out of sorts
And considered
How to usher in
First light of a new bore.

New Haven Manor

Lovely maniac
lives in the Home down the avenue from ours.
Face sticks out of the ground
floor windows,
sings to passersby, "you never know what will happen"
and other such taradiddle.
Heaps of white sticks
Nicotine Lane
Conifers, humane,
in the front entrance,
kept a distance
in the past, and still do.
Rambling raconteurs
rubbing their eyes of phosphenes,
unfortunate souls
inhabiting the place
chatting up old
acquaintances in their craniums.
Stupefyingly,
contentment creases their faces.
The poorest on this street
bereft of neediness,
the endless hunts for wellbeing
that so oppress
their coherent counterparts.
How unfortunate, really, can they be
with stray cats slinking around their heads and
only nonsensical
mice to catch.
How handicapped could they have been
when fancies ran just as
rampant through the din –
so erratically –
in the minds of all the other households
on the block that never knew Sanity.

Resistance

Been briefed on grief and love lost
Disappointment faded
Video games to numb out the pain
Numbness a blessing
Anticipated.
Row your boat straight down – not up –
The Stream, over
Rapids drifting, drifting
Murkiness settling
Gloriousness unfolding
If not now, then at God's ending.
Desist white-knuckling this
With useless hubris
And demands that your plans be
Established.
Broken animatronics
Won't speed up the process
That's a promise
But honest –
Life gets better at the start of surrender.

Too Close to Home

The wind brushed past my face
with its full nonchalance,
as if
questioning my presence
in that place.

It was yesterday all over again,
the prior night's moon chained to the blue one
above my contemplative head.

For what purpose
would I leave suburbia and my warm bed . . .
to catch a glimpse of a stale lifetime?

The dimple on my cheek made a quick appearance.
No one noticed,
I almost missed it myself.

And when the past finally arrived,
no reaction came to her face
and none to mine.
Could it be
she didn't recognize herself?

We both froze,
rabbits in a trap.
Too late.
The door of her house met its frame,
and a shadow passed over those cheap paper shades.
Old rabbits die hard.

A Towel Thrown In

Here is a person who has managed to find
An answer so clear to get out of the bind,
And here is his nemesis dressed as an Ordeal
To convince him to forfeit all he knows to be real.

To convince him to forfeit all solutions he's had,
A nemesis cloaked in problem-stitched plaid
Makes an appearance to tighten the quandary,
Until here is a person more high strung than laundry.

Apple of The I

My Destiny, the card read
They leaned back and laughed
And won.
I thought I felt what was going on,
But I was wrong.
Since then
The self's been shed
Since forgiveness was supposed to be the scent
That the violet spread
On the heel that had crushed it.
And when
The peel's been discarded,
Regret disregarded
As a sick snake that left its skin behind,
There are still fault lines in heaven for reminders
To crawl in
But to damage? Not a chance.
I lost – I win.

Imago

Poring over this story – misbegotten, the words shorn.
Pondering what may well be
the worst of the lovelorn~
And it's funny to observe the purest truth, long forsworn;
Who knew you have to die
before you can be born ꙮ

B. Miller is a twenty-year-old etymology enthusiast living on Long Island, NY. Much of her writing is prompted by her experiences and those of others. She is a proud Orthodox Jew.